Pastor Ollie Simmons White is a native of Colleton County. She is the daughter of the late Franklin and Ella Mae Simmons. She graduated from Colleton High School. Pastor Ollie White is the Spiritual mother of many who seek her advice on a regular basis.

Pastor White accepted Christ in 1968. The Lord placed a higher calling on her in 1981. Since that time, she has spoken in other cities and states, such as Waco and San Antonio, Texas, and Ocala, Florida. Ollie White was led by God to begin a family support group that meets once a week at her home. She is previously the author of two books entitled "Against all Odds, Determined to Succeed" and "I Live to Tell the Story".

God has given Pastor White many experiences and the gifts of healing. Her spiritual gift of discernment has led many people to victory in the name of Jesus. Throughout her faith walk, this anointed gift as led her to assume many titles within the faith community such as Mother Prophetess, Prayer Warrior, Spiritual Leader, amongst others.

Pastor Ollie White is currently the head pastor at Faith and Action Ministries located in Walterboro, SC. She was ordained as a pastor in 2011 and established Faith and Action Ministries in 2012. Faith and Action Ministries is dedicated to serving the Lord and teaching faith in the Colleton County area where the church has two locations.

Pastor White loves to minister to the broken, battered, bruised and the homeless. She is an anointed woman of God who will witness to anybody, anywhere. She is a woman of great faith and walk with God. Her testimonies range from raising all of her siblings at the tender age of 19 after her mother died, to building her two-story house starting with $3.79.

Faith, Action, & Determination

Pastor Ollie M. White

authorHOUSE®

AuthorHouse™
1663 Liberty Drive
Bloomington, IN 47403
www.authorhouse.com
Phone: 833-262-8899

Published by AuthorHouse 07/31/2024

ISBN: 979-8-8230-3068-7 (sc)
ISBN: 979-8-8230-3067-0 (e)

Library of Congress Control Number: 2024915371

Print information available on the last page.

Prelude

Readers, you will find that this book and my other two books are full of many true faith stories of how trusting in God results in happy endings!

Early in my adult life, I realized that I had to start writing and become an author. I had been through so much in my life, and had many stories to tell—stories of survival, of true, strong faith, of action, and of determination. There were also stories of victory in the midst of the storm. I knew that sooner or later, I would have to start writing a book. I could not get over so many things that happened in my past. I kept putting it off because I could not find the time to write a book. I was too busy for my own good. My main job was working as a teacher's assistant. I also went to the beach to clean houses on the weekend and sometimes waited tables in the evening as a part-time job. I held down three jobs, yet somehow, I managed to attend church services and take care of my children. I knew all the time that many other people needed to hear my story.

Unshakable Faith

Faith, Action, and Determination

God Made It Happen

Sometimes we have to take a bad fall before we can get up and head in the right direction. At my full-time job, at the end of the day, I was helping a student gather her belongings. The little girl was a car rider, and her name was being called on the intercom. At the end of each day, we would put the classroom chairs upside down on the tables. Somehow, on this particular day, one of the chairs was partially under the table. I stumbled over that chair, and I fell backward against a table. My back was seriously injured, but I was able to get up. I kept reporting to school, trying to work in spite of the pain. I had to bring a report back to work from my doctor stating that I was OK to work. I did not want to quit working, but the pain medication was not helping much at all.

Eventually, the doctor sent a letter stating that I could no longer keep doing the same job; he said maybe I could do light duty. The supervisor told me that they would allow me to file papers and make phone calls to parents whenever there was a change in schedules or anything of that nature. The doctor told me from the beginning that I would need back surgery. He said that fall did a lot of damage to my back. After about two months, I was called into the supervisor's office. I was hoping to hear some good news. When I entered into the office, I was told that as of that very day, I no longer had a job. I was told that they could no longer keep me on light duty. I was lost for words. For a moment, there was nothing but complete silence. When they asked me if I had anything to say, once I got myself together, I said, "Yes, I do. I thank you for trying to keep me on the job, but now that I no longer have a job, I do have a book to write." I felt that this was God's way of giving me the time and opportunity to begin writing and telling my story.

A Big, Big Storm

The meeting with my supervisor took place at the end of the school day. I remember asking the supervisor to let me leave a few minutes early. I did not want to tell all my coworkers that I had just been terminated, and I would not be there anymore. I was not ready for that. I felt like I had just lost everything and every friend I ever had. Every step I took toward my vehicle, I was asking the Lord, "Where do I go from here?" There was no need to look for another job because I had an injury that would not allow me to work anywhere. Despite what was going on, I knew God had a plan for my life (Jeremiah 29:11 KJV). What would you do if you hit rock bottom? The answer is bounce back. God has something better for you. When you feel like all hope is gone, have faith in God. Put your faith into action, be determined, and no matter what, trust God. I am reminded of Mark 11:24: "Therefore, I say unto you, what things soever ye desire, when ye pray, believe that ye receive them and ye shall have them."

However, my back pain continued to get worse. I finally had to have the surgery on my back. I could not put it off any longer. That was another long and very painful situation. I was very sick for a long time. I could tell that the enemy was working overtime trying to break me down, but I thank God for Isaiah 59:19: "When the enemy shall come in like a flood, the spirit of the Lord shall lift up a standard against him." As I began to recover from the back surgery, I was ready to write my book. I thought it would be fun finally getting started, and I was looking forward to sharing my experiences. As I began to write my life story, I had to be reminded of so many painful things.

The title of my first book was *Against All Odds: Determined to Succeed*.

I had no intentions of writing more than one book. I felt like one book would be enough. After my first book was published, it was not long before I realized there was another book to write. There was so much more to write about. There were so many stories to tell. These stories would inspire and encourage many other people. I have been told many times that my first book needs to be a movie. I already know that, but I had no way of getting the book where it needed to go. I did not have the money to promote my book. I would love for the world to not only read my story but also see it. Believe it or not, God still works miracles. I am a living witness.

There is nothing too hard for God. God has no respect of person. He never slumbers or sleeps. I kept hearing the voice of the Lord say, "Keep writing." I could never write enough books to exemplify how awesome God is. It is unexplainable! My daughter said if you can explain it, then God did not do it. I enjoy the feedback when people let me know that they really enjoy reading my books, especially when someone tells me the book was inspirational. I don't mind letting people know that every day was not a good day, but I trusted God no matter what. There were times when bad news hit me so suddenly and unexpectedly, I thought I would not be able to get over it. This happened over and over again. Before I could get past one thing, something else would overlap it. I could tell that the enemy was working overtime trying to stop me, but I learned to trust God no matter what. Before I ever picked up a pen to write the first paragraph, I already knew how to trust God because the Lord has proven himself to me so many times.

Walking with God by Faith

My walk of faith in God began many years ago, during a time when I did not know what faith in God was. As a small child, I did not understand what it meant to walk with the Lord, but I knew something was missing in my little life. There were times when I wanted to talk to someone about the things that were going on in my mind, but I knew or thought that no one would understand. My little cousins always thought I was a weird little person. I would hear voices that no one else could hear. The voices would always sound sweet and soft. I was never afraid of anything. The voices always made me feel a sense of security. I was searching for answers. I could not understand why I did not fit in anywhere. What was wrong with me? Why did I have to be a misfit? As a small child, I would wander off into the woods across from where I lived. I would look for a stump or a tree that had fallen down to sit on and meditate. There is something about that stump; it was my secret closet. I was not afraid of anything because I felt like I was not alone. I knew that I had a friend who would protect me. Although I did not know who he was at that time, I felt like if I ever needed him, he would be there for me. To this very day, he has proven to be the best friend I've ever had.

While I was going through those changes, I hoped to meet or find someone who could help me understand. I felt like I was in my own little world, all by myself. I liked to sit on the floor with my back against the wall. I wanted to be all alone. I did not like to be distracted. I was trying to see what the next thing would be. I did not know what was going on, but I felt like something good was coming out of this.

I didn't understand the potential of the power of God because I did not grow up in the church. I did not have a chance to hear what the Word of God said until later in life when a little old lady in the neighborhood started taking me to church. I still felt like I was so different from all the other children in the community because I was the only child who would cry to go to church. I never felt like a normal child. There was a question in my mind every day: *Why just me?* It was like I was dreaming. I was looking forward to going to church because I felt as if someone at the church would help me understand why I was so different.

I felt as if I had to prepare for a long, hard journey. I did not know at the time, but Habakkuk 2:3 states, "The vision is yet for an appointed time but at the end, it shall speak and not lie. Though it tarry, wait for it, because it will surely come. It will not tarry." Somehow, I knew I was made for more.

When I was ten years old, I would go on long walks. My mother lived in the city of Walterboro and my grandmother lived in the country (or what we called the Great Swamp). The Great Swamp was approximately three miles from Walterboro. On a good day when the weather was warm and sunny, I would put some of my clothes in a bag and leave home, walking to the country. My mother did not seem to be worried about me.

Never Alone

On my long walk to the country, I never felt like I was walking alone. I felt like someone was walking right beside me. Every now and then, I thought I heard a little voice that made me feel like I was not alone. The voice was audible, but I could hear it in my spirit.

Sometimes, I was fortunate enough to catch a ride, but not too often. Whenever someone would stop to pick me up, it would always be someone I knew or someone who knew my grandmother. I have always been very grateful for everything anyone did to help me. You would think that I would be very happy to catch a ride, but whenever someone gave me a ride, that meant I would have to leave my best friend behind. I missed him. It did not bother me at all when I could walk with my best friend. I could hardly wait until the driver put me out at the head of the dirt road that led to my grandmother's house. My grandmother lived about one quarter of a mile down a dusty dirt road. The greatest thing about being put out at the head of the dirt road was the fact that my invisible best friend would be waiting there for me. I could not see my friend, but I knew he was always there. He was a true friend, sticking closer than a sister or brother.

My grandmother's house was surrounded by her sons, daughters, and many grandchildren. I remember hearing the tales walking down that dusty dirt road. My uncles used to tell my little cousins and me about the bears that supposedly lived in the woods on the dirt road. Every now and then, someone would say that he or she saw what we called a "hog bear" coming out of the woods. I don't know about the other children, but I did not believe anything about that story. I also felt like if the bears did come out of the woods, my best friend would not let the bears harm me.

Little did I know there really was a friend that I could not see but could depend on. As I grew up, I found out who my best friend really was. I had a chance to meet him in a real way. He is so much more than just a friend; he is the son of God, the Savior of the whole world. He is a healer. He is a deliverer. He is a keeper. I did not know that he was keeping me for such a time as this—a time when I needed him the most. I just did not understand. He is so much more than you and I could ever imagine. He is the giver of every good and perfect gift. His name is Jesus. He will never leave you or forsake you. He will be with you always. I am sorry for anyone who doesn't know him.

I never had to walk back from the country. My mother would have someone bring her to my grandmother's house. My mother would say, "Ollie, it is time to go home now." Even though I was never ready to go home, I did not say a word. The strangest thing about this is my mother had six sisters and three brothers alive at the time, and I still cannot believe that not one of them ever said a word to me about walking alone. They never asked me who came with me or who gave me a ride. Maybe they also knew that I was not alone. Unfortunately, not one of my mother's siblings lived to see or witness me become a minister.

Sometimes, I wondered if others knew about my friend. If someone had asked about him, he or she would have had to listen to this long story about my invisible friend who is always with me. For some reason, no one ever asked me questions and I am not sure why. Maybe they did not want to hear the story, did not believe in someone they could not see, or were afraid to hear about him. All I know is that he was real then, and he is very much real now. Whether or not anyone else believes it, he is real to me. I will never trade him for anyone or anything that I can see or touch. Sometimes when we are on a long journey, we grow tired, but we have to keep walking. We have to keep pushing and praying until something happens. We need to know that God is with us wherever we go, whether anyone else understands it or not. God will finish what he started in your life.

Taking Me Away

Most of my life, I have been tossed around like a ball, not knowing what the next day would bring. My father was never in my life. He was a migrant worker. He would stop in to see my family and me every now and then, whenever he was passing through the area. No one knew when he would be stopping by. I am not sure if anyone in my family was in contact with him, but I can't help but believe that someone was. I believe my father made a special trip to take me from my mother. I believe someone told my father that I would leave home and walk all the way to the country by myself. He asked my mother if he could take me to visit his brother across town. Even though he did not tell my mother when he would bring me back, my mother trusted him. She thought he would have me back home before dark. Once we arrived at my uncle's, my father told me that he would be back to get me. I never saw him again. My father was happy because I was with his brother and his sister-in-law. I was not happy at all. I missed my mother, and I knew she missed me. I had no contact with my mother. When I was old enough to walk away, that's what I did. My father later died in Florida. My uncle had his body brought home to South Carolina.

At an early age, I had to learn to forgive. When I went back home, my mother made sure that I learned how to do the things that a mother does for her children. I had some mighty big shoes to fill.

Now I am beginning to understand why no one could help me figure out all of the complicated things that took place in my childhood. God does not always call those who qualify, but he always qualifies those whom he calls.

No one knew that my mother would pass away while I was a

teenager, and I would have to raise my four younger siblings. There I was: nineteen years old, with two children of my own and raising my siblings. I decided to keep all of my siblings together and raise them as my own. I believe that is what the Lord was preparing me for. He wanted me to hear his voice and feel his presence. I had to be different. I had to be a single parent with six children.

Finally, the pieces to the lifelong puzzle were beginning to come together. Habakkuk 2:3 says, "The vision is yet for an appointed time, but at the end it shall speak and not lie, though it tarry, wait for it because it will surely come, it will not tarry." Things were beginning to make sense to me. I realized there was a call on my life all of those years. I just needed to answer the call. At first, I tried everything that I could think of to avoid answering the call to ministry. I knew that pastoring a church would certainly be a full-time job and that I would be taking on a lot of responsibility. Even though I love praying for and ministering to people, I knew that would mean no rest for the weary, and I was right about that.

I told the Lord that I was already carrying too heavy a burden. I tried to bargain with the Lord. I told him my heart was broken into pieces and that I was getting too old to take on such a task. I also told him that I might not have enough help or support. I had nightmares when I thought about everyone wanting to have his or her way. I did not want the headache of trying to please everyone. I thought about how people would walk away when or if things did not go their way. I had to remind myself that all excuses were nailed to the cross. Believe me when I tell you that I had to repent for not wanting to do what God called me to do.

One of the greatest things that ever happened to me was when I read Jeremiah 29:11. It let me know there were "thoughts I think towards you saith the Lord. Thoughts of peace and not of evil to give you an expected end." The Lord was also letting me know that if I needed him for anything to seek him. Jeremiah 29:12 says, "Then shall ye call upon me and ye shall go and pray unto me and I will answer you."

When I was a child, I had no one to teach or tell me that I could pray and call on the Lord for an answer. I was searching for answers in all the wrong places. Jeremiah 29:13 let me know that if I seek him, I will find him when I search for him with all of my heart. I never walked alone; the Lord was always there. I could feel that someone was there. I felt pressured to get started. I prayed and asked the Lord to strengthen me as I began a fifty-day consecration. I went upstairs every night. I began to anoint myself, the stairs, the windows, the chairs, and everything else in my sight. I took my Bible and a notebook. I prayed, read the Bible, and wrote down everything that the Lord had given me. I could feel the anointing on my life growing stronger. I wondered where all this was going.

At one point, I felt like I was losing my mind. Then I remembered going into the woods to hear from God. During the course of the fifty days, I was very careful and prayerful about what I did and who I communicated with. I made sacrifices and planted seeds. I just wanted to be sure that I was pleasing God in all my ways. Proverbs 3:6 says, "In all thy ways acknowledge him and he shall direct thy paths." I remember becoming very excited toward the end of the fifty days. I knew something great was about to happen.

On the morning of the fiftieth day, I woke up with the idea to have a service in the upper room. I called the people whom I felt led to call. I told them there would be a Pentecostal outpouring service at my home at 6:00 p.m. that day. I made sure to emphasize that they should not be late. I planned everything just as the Lord instructed. People started arriving around 5:30 p.m. Shortly after 6:00 p.m., I locked the door. Thirty-three people attended. If you were not there, this story would be hard to believe. People came running to experience this! Even my children's ninety-year-old grandmother was in attendance. She said, "I want to be there!" My son-in-law tried to help get her to the top of the stairs so that she could be a part of it. I was next in line, and he was behind her. I noticed him struggling to keep her on her feet. He said to her, "Come on, Grandma. I got you." I did not know why she could not step over into the upper room.

Finally, my son-in-law was able to get my children's grandmother up the stairs. Excitement was in the air. The presence of the Lord was strong. That service was both strange and highly anointed. Everyone who attended the service wondered what was going to happen next. We began to praise the Lord. We read scriptures and sang songs. As I told everyone when I called them, it was truly a Pentecostal outpouring service. We were all of one accord. I was reminded many times of Acts 2:2, which states, "Suddenly there came a sound from heaven as of a rushing mighty wind, and it filled all the house where they were sitting." This actually happened during the service, and for some reason, I thought I was the only one that felt the wind in the upper room. Later that week, I went to visit Grandma at her home. She said to me, "Ollie, I got to tell you something. Do you know why I could not get up the stairs that day? I felt a strong wind blowing me. It was a good feeling." The upper room experience took place about thirteen years ago and people are still talking about it today.

Getting Me Ready for Ministry

The Lord was laying a foundation for this ministry. A great work began in my home. For two years, my family and I met at my home in the upper room every Saturday at 6:00 p.m. Everyone was excited about coming together in the upper room. Sometimes, we would have guests from out of town with their children. We experienced the move of God just like it was described in the book of Acts. When the Holy Spirit fell upon everyone in the room, our services became very anointed. Before long, we outgrew the upper room. Children were sitting in every corner and on the stairway.

The Lord was preparing me to launch out into the deep. I felt that the Lord was up to something great. I just did not know how great. One day, I went into the upper room all alone to pray. The Lord spoke to me about finding a building to start a church. I had been preaching, teaching, praying, and laying hands on the sick, and God would bring it to pass. I can truly say that finding a building was the only thing left to do. The Lord was so busy using me and letting me know that I was ready to be a pastor. I could not focus on finding a building. I was happy with our Saturday evening services. The Lord was letting me know that it was time for me to move on. I am reminded of the story in 1 Kings chapter 17 when the Lord spoke to Elijah saying that the brook dried up. It was time to move on. There was greater work to be done.

God Saw the Best in Me

During this time, I sat under an awesome man of God, Bishop Taylor. He asked me, "How long are you going to run from this work that God has called you to?" He said, "I know the Lord told you because he keeps telling me." At the time, I was a licensed minister. Bishop Taylor said to me, "I need to get you licensed as a pastor." I cannot say that I was surprised. He said, "We need to schedule an ordination service just for you." I humbled myself, answered the call, and Bishop Taylor scheduled the date to ordain me as a pastor. He made several trips to my house prior to the service. Bishop wanted to prepare me for the task set before me. Many people had already recognized the call on my life. Family and friends came from far and near to see me finally answer the call as a leader. They all said, "It's about time." After the ordination service, I felt led to sit under Bishop for another year. After a while, Bishop and I began to look for a building for my church. We looked everywhere and could not find a building.

Every time I thought I found a building to start my church, something went wrong. This happened numerous times. If I tried to explain what happened, and how many buildings I looked at, I would have to write another book. Despite all of the unsuccessful searches, I could not give up. Quitting was not an option. I kept thinking that a quitter will never win, and a winner never quits. I kept praying and standing on the Word of God. Mark 11:24 says, "Therefore, I say unto you, what things soever ye desire when ye pray, believe that ye receive them and ye shall have them."

It finally came to pass. One day while out riding and writing down phone numbers, I decided to pull over in the parking lot of a funeral home to use my cell phone. I was attempting to call the contact numbers for the buildings that I saw. I was sitting directly in front of the sign that displayed the phone number of a funeral home. I sat there in my car for about thirty minutes and then I thought to myself, *Why don't I call this number and ask someone about renting the sanctuary of this place? I pass by here all of the time and I never see any cars or any funerals here. Maybe this building is available. After all, what do I have to lose?*

To my surprise, someone answered the phone. Before the conversation began, I started to feel like my prayers had been answered. I did not know, but a woman was inside the building and asked me to come in. The first thing that she said to me was, "You must be the person that I asked the Lord to send. I want to rent the sanctuary to a trustworthy person. Would you be interested?" She then said, "Come on, let's sit on the pulpit." Her name was Miss Linda, and she and I sat on the pulpit for about an hour. We discussed and finalized a lease agreement. I was so overwhelmed with excitement that I did not think to inspect everything in the building, like the heat and air units. That was a mistake! However, God had blessed me with a place to get my church ministry started. The building's sanctuary had enough things in place for me to begin right away.

Miracles in the Funeral Home

I asked everybody to bring an electric heater to help heat the building during services. Despite circumstances, trials, and tribulations, people kept on coming. Sometimes it would be so cold that people would sit with their coats and hats on. Yet I felt that God would get the glory out of this. I had to be able to see through the eyes of faith. I had to have faith, put faith in action, and believe. Somehow, I knew that the Lord had great things in store for us. Many times, I had to encourage myself in the Lord. I told the saints to be encouraged. I told them we were going to press our way through.

I believed it was because the people had seen the great work that the Lord had done when we were having church at my house. I believed they were willing to run on and see what the end would be. We kept on praying and praising the Lord. Sometimes, our offering was just enough to pay our rent and to keep our church doors open for services. We held services several weeks before I opened the doors for members to join the church. I had friends who supported and fellowshipped with us on a regular basis. When I found a building and opened the church, I was happy to know that my friends kept on coming. Some of them were members of other churches, but they still came to support. Slowly but surely, the church began to grow, and people began to join. Some of them stayed and some of them left, but we also had enough members to survive. I never felt led to close the doors. I was determined to continue pressing forward with the members I had.

Shortly after I opened the church, we had a thirty-day revival. We had a different speaker each night. People came from all over. I learned a valuable lesson from that revival. Everyone has his or her own unique way of doing things. Every service was great. Every sermon was inspiring and encouraging. I learned that I had better put on the whole armor of God. I learned that God had many great works for me to do. The revival left me anxious for the next thing God had in store for. I wanted more. I wanted to do more. My years of spiritual experiences under sound leadership prepared me to lead my ministry with faith and obedience and continue to grow. I am grateful for the teaching that I have received from great leaders. I thank God for tough love and being able to take chastisement and correction. Bishop Taylor did not play with us. He would set us down in a heartbeat. I am a living witness.

Bishop spent a lot of time pouring into me and preparing me to start up my ministry. I believe Bishop Taylor felt that his time was winding up. I believe he knew that he was about to go home to be with the Lord. It was a blessing that he was still teaching me new things in ministry. I learned so much from him over the period of forty-two years. I raised all of my children in his church. He was a great mentor. He could almost tell me what was on my mind. I worked very closely with him for many years. Every time Bishop would give me some advice or teach me how to do something, he would always ask me, "Do you have any questions?" Bishop also said, "I am not worried about you. I know you are going to be a great little pastor." He never walked away without assuring me that I would be just fine. I am just fine because I learned from the best. Bishop Taylor preached my anniversary every year until he died. I never got a chance to preach for Bishop on one of his anniversary services, but I was glad to be in the pulpit with him. I was like the man at the pool in John 5:7; every time I thought it was my time, someone else would step up before me. However, I was glad to make remarks for five minutes. I was glad to be in the number. After Bishop went home to be with the Lord, I still found myself picking up the telephone to call him.

Growing Pain

I am so glad that I don't wear my feelings on my sleeve. If I did, I never would have made it because I have been crushed many times. Pain, struggles, heartbreaks, disappointments, and rejections are some of the things that I endured, and they shaped me into who I am. These things helped make me tough. How you go through life is very important. If you can take it, you can make it. In order for you to lead, you must be willing to bleed. My struggles taught me that hearing the voice of the Lord before you make any decisions is important. If I were to write about all the painful things that I made it through, I would have to write an endless book. I would not know where to start. I would always look back on when I was searching for a church and how I experienced so many setbacks and disappointments. Every time I thought about it, I got happy about finally being settled into our own church. It seems like the bottom would fall out and I would find myself riding all over the county looking for a building all over again.

While we were leasing our first building, we had a lease agreement suitable for our budget. We had a month-to-month agreement. The owner kept increasing the rent and adding other expenses. I felt like we were being driven out. While the rent was rising rapidly, we had to prepare to leave. The rent became more than four times higher than it was when we first started using the building. The sad part about that was I really loved that building and I did not want to leave.

The Lord worked many miracles in that building right before our very eyes. God turned the funeral home into a healing and deliverance center. Souls were saved, and people were healed, delivered, and set free. Many addictions and bad habits were broken. I never wavered in my faith. I felt like wherever I went, the anointing would be there with me.

The word of God lets me know that he will never leave me or forsake me, that he will be with me always, even until the end of the world. I began to pray and seek God because I was not about to the throw in the towel. Seeing the hands of God determined to move, it was time to put faith into action. I prayed and asked the Lord where he wanted us to be. It was not long before we found a building not far from where we were. For some reason, that building was vacant for a long time, but I did not see it. I know that God had that building in reserve for Faith and Action Ministries.

Of course, there was a fight, but it was a fixed fight. Everybody told me that there was no way I would be allowed to put a church in that building. For some reason, many were interested in the location, but no one could get it. The building had the lights on. It had hot and cold running water. It had heat and air, a kitchen, a fellowship hall, a balcony, and a patio. That building had everything we needed. The enemy tried everything he could to keep us from using this building. The inspectors kept coming up with reasons why we couldn't open the building as a church. We leased the building, made payments for eleven months, and we were not allowed to even use the bathroom. I told the saints that we were going to do what the Word says. Based on the sixth chapter of Joshua, I was not about to give up. I decided that we would march around that building for seven days. I went to the hardware store and bought seven little wooden sticks and some thumbtacks. I made seven victory signs. We marched around the building one time. For the first six days, we walked each day at 7:00 p.m. Each day when we made a complete circle and came back to the front of the building, I would put a victory sign in the ground.

On the seventh day, we marched around seven times, reading faith scriptures, singing victory songs, carrying babies in our arms, pushing strollers, praying, and trusting God. Once we completed seven rounds on the seventh day, we rejoiced as if we already owned the building. People passing by were looking at us like they were trying to figure out what was going on.

There was a little lady living next door to the building. She sat on her porch and watched us as we marched around the building each day. She watched us put the victory signs in the ground. One day, she called me and said, "I don't understand something about these little victory signs. When rain come down so hard, the signs look like they will be torn up, but when the sun come out, the signs stand back up again as if they never got wet. I think that is so good. I believe everything is going to work in your favor."

I left the signs standing there, I prayed the prayer of faith, and I said, "Lord, I am standing on the promises of your written word." I went on my way. I trusted that God would work it out. A few weeks later, I received a phone call. The person let me know that if I still wanted the building, I could have it, and setting it up as a church would not be a problem. Shortly thereafter, we moved into our building and made it the house of worship for Faith and Action Ministries.

Nobody Told Me That the Road Would Be Easy

I experienced many shipwrecks. I was never promised smooth sailing, but I always had a safe landing. It takes a well made-up mind to serve the Lord. My mind is made up. I am on my way up; I'm going to hold my head up and I am going all the way with the Lord. Once you have gone through the valley, you will appreciate the mountain top. Faith and Action Ministries was built and founded on prayer, faith, healing, deliverance, and tough love. Our ministry is an example of faith, action, and determination. Many people have come through Faith and Action Ministries and were healed and delivered. To God be the glory for the things he has done. I want everyone to know that God can, and he will, answer prayers. God specializes in things that seem impossible. I love it when everyone has given up on a situation, then God turns around and makes it happen. I thank God for supernatural favor.

Speak, Lord, for Thy Servant Heareth: One Hundred Days of Prayer

I had just returned from the hospital after having a total hip replacement. I was sitting in a corner at the church when I heard a still, small voice down in my spirit. I know it was the Lord speaking to me. He said, "One hundred days of prayer." I thought the one hundred days of prayer would be something personal, because I had been praying for directions about taking the church to the next level. I did not say anything to the church members immediately. I began to question God for instructions. I knew there was more to come, even if it was just for me. I waited for him to speak again. The very next Sunday, while standing at the altar in prayer at the beginning of the service, I heard the voice of the Lord again. He said, "One hundred days of prayer." The spirit was high, and everyone was praising the Lord in loud voices. He said, "Tell everybody." My daughter-in-law had the microphone because she was the prayer leader. I had to wait until she said amen. I was excited about hearing from the Lord about the one hundred days of prayer. I thought to myself, *How am I going to tell the church we are going into prayer for one hundred days? My congregation is used to thirty days or twenty-one days of prayer because we have done that many times.* As soon as the altar prayer was over, I asked for the microphone, and I told the church what the Lord told me. To my surprise, everyone was in agreement. They stood up on their feet and said, "Amen Pastor," as if they were waiting to hear those words. I knew God was up to something, so I wanted to do everything just right. I wanted to be sure I was using the right scriptures for such an awesome assignment. I knew there was even more. When the Lord gives you something to do, he will also test your faith, like he did with Abraham with Isaac. This is to see if you will do anything that he tells you to do.

I began to seek the Lord like never before. I did not want to miss him. There was a lot of gang activity and violence going on in this small town. Sometimes there were two or three funerals every day. Things became really bad. If there ever been a time to pray, that was the time. I could hardly wait to get started. I had nothing to lose. I felt like there was at least one other thing that needed to be done.

Many people in this area were receiving refund checks from our utility company. It took a while for my check to come, but it finally came. I was happy that I could move forward with my plans to spend it like I wanted to. However, the Lord tested my faith. The Holy Spirit told me to cash the check, take the tithe out of it, and give the rest of it to Carolyn. I knew that I was being tested and, like Abraham and many others in the Bible, I obeyed God. I had left Carolyn's house after giving her the money, and the Holy Spirit said to me, "The scripture for the one hundred days of prayer is 2 Chronicles 7:14." I could not remember just what the verse said, so I pulled over to the side of the road and took out my Bible. I took my time reading the scripture and I was so relieved that God had provided me with the theme verse for the prayer. Just remember that this was before the coronavirus.

I was so overwhelmed; I could not move on. I had to take the time to thank the Lord for what he was doing in me, and what he was about to do. When I read that scripture, I felt like a new door was about to open, and so it did. The relationship that I have with the Lord is worth more than any amount of money. I would give anything just to be able to hear from the Lord. All doubts were settled. We didn't know what exactly the one hundred days of prayer was for, and we were not aware of any pandemic or anything like that. Only God knew what was about to happen.

We started prayer immediately. We prayed at the church twice a day for one hundred days straight. We prayed every day at noon and at 7:00 p.m. The Lord said to tell everybody, so we placed poster signs up and passed out flyers all over Walterboro (our city). I went to our local newspaper and met with someone there. Ms. McCall published an article in the weekly paper without delay. She and everyone else in this town knew that prayer was very much needed. Ms. McCall ran the article every week until I informed her that the one hundred days was over. I ministered twice a day for one hundred days. I was hoping that everyone would come to be a witness of what the Lord was about to do. The Lord moved mightily in each service. There was no question about whether or not the Lord ordained the one hundred days of prayer. We read 2 Chronicles 7:14 in every prayer session. It reads, "If my people which are called by name will humble themselves and pray and seek my face and turn from their wicked ways, then will I hear from heaven and forgive their sin and heal their land."

God continued to prove himself to us many times. The members of our church believed in taking God at his word. As soon as we began the one hundred days of prayer, the violence in the city stopped at once. Not one person was murdered in the city of Walterboro during the one hundred days of prayer. We would say, "Speak Lord, thy servant is listening." The prayer was powerful. Not only did God heal the land, but he also healed many people. He saved souls. Truly, the mission was accomplished. I will never forget the great work and the miracles that were performed during those daily prayer sessions. The Lord has truly blessed our church. People kept on coming every day. Some of the members had to work during the day, but they could hardly wait for the night session. Some of them were there one hundred days without missing. Not only did we pray and read 2 Chronicles 7:14, we also read other scriptures. Every day, we asked, "Is there anything too hard for God?" (Jeremiah 32:27). The answer is "no." In 2 Chronicles 7:13, the Lord declares, "If I shut up heaven that there be no rain or if I command the locusts to devour the land, or if I send the pestilence among my people." The Lord was letting us know that we didn't have anything to lose if we served him. I reminded the prayer group every day in my message that God was preparing us for something, and we needed to be prayed up. We had no idea that we would be facing a pandemic in a few months. No one wanted to see the prayer sessions come to an end.

When the reporter from our local newspaper heard that we were about to end the one hundred days of prayer, she came by the church. We were in the noonday prayer. She took some pictures, interviewed about fourteen people, and recorded their testimonies. She asked them what they had to say about the prayer. I really enjoyed listening as they gave their testimonies and praise reports. They told how the Lord was blessing them since the prayer started. The local newspaper published a full page of testimonies and pictures for the public to see. The headline in big bold letters was "They Called, God Answered!" Usually, churches take up offerings at any type of service to cover the cost of electricity and other facility usage. However, we never took up any offering during the one hundred days of prayer, because it was not about the money. No amount of money could be better than the work that God did in those one hundred days of prayer. It will never be forgotten.

After the one hundred days of prayer, it was like miracles were falling from heaven. It was like finding and unlocking hidden treasures. I am reminded of Isaiah 45:13, which reads as follows.

> Thus saith the Lord to his anointed, to Cyrus, whose right hand I have holden, to subdue nations before him; and I will loose the loins of kings to open before him the two levied gates; and the gates shall not be shut; I will go before thee and make the crooked places straight. I will break in pieces the gates of brass and cut in sunder the bars of iron, and I will give thee the treasures of darkness, and hidden riches of secret places that thou mayest know that I, the Lord which call tee by thy name, am the God of Israel.

Coronavirus Just around the Corner

Coronavirus was not heard of yet. We were persistent in prayer and standing on faith in God's Word. The one hundred days of prayer started August 12, 2019 and ended on November 19, 2019. About four months later, the news media and everybody started talking about COVID-19. All the hospitals were filled to capacity. People were dying so fast that funerals were held every day. What caught my attention more than anything was the fact that everybody everywhere, on TV, on the internet, and locally, was using the same scripture that the Lord gave me. I noticed the scripture became popular even before the virus was heard of. Only God knows the future and what is about to happen. We serve an awesome God.

Another scripture we read every day was James 5:13–18. I never heard much about these scriptures until COVID-19 appeared. After the virus came, suddenly, every preacher on television and everywhere was talking about 2 Chronicles 7:14. By the time the coronavirus came on the scene, I was so prayed up, because I kept praying and thanking God for what he continued to do. I know many people thought I was crazy, but I just could not be afraid of the virus. I did everything that was asked of me to obey the laws of the land and to be safe, but I was not afraid.

My mother once told me that I had to be a crazy person. She said anybody in their right mind would be afraid of some things sometimes. When she said that to me, I did not know who was behind the voices that I had been hearing all those years. Now that I know of the Holy Spirit, I am really crazy about him. I believe I know what to be afraid of. If I was afraid of everything, I would have been cast down and destroyed many years ago. I would have been afraid to trust God. When he speaks, I will do just what he says. I know his voice; I will listen and obey. "Speak Lord, I am listening." I cannot be afraid and do the work that God has called me to do. Many times, I had to stand firm and be bold and very courageous. Many times, I had no one to stand up for me or with me, if I was afraid to stand alone. I have overcome many dangerous toils and snares. Grace has brought me safe this far and grace will lead me on because I trust God. I have gone up against many giants that others were afraid to fight. The battle was fought, and the victory was won. Everybody can't be afraid; somebody needs to stand with boldness and trust God. God needs some more Davids to bring down some Goliaths. You don't need to have a whole lot of stones; you just need the right rock, which is Jesus. The antidote for fear is faith.

Crazy Faith

The word *crazy* can be defined in more than one way. When it comes to believing God for things that seem impossible, yes, I am that kind of crazy. The Word of God declares in the gospel of St. John 14:14, "If ye shall ask anything in my name, I will do it." I am crazy enough to believe what St. John 14:13 says: "And whatsoever ye shall ask in my name, that will I do, that the father may be glorified in the son."

I believe that faith without works is dead. I can recall many instances where, if I did not put faith in action, sad would have been my case. I realize that everyone has a measure of faith, but not everyone has the gift of faith. I thank the Lord because I do have the gift. I know that faith comes by hearing and by hearing the Word of God. I teach on faith in my church all of the time. I can hardly make it through a sermon without sharing a faith story. I try to build the saints' faith by telling them some of the things the Lord has done in my life when I trusted him with my crazy faith. Sometimes, when I am sharing great faith stories, I will see someone looking at me like a deer at headlights. I don't understand why people can't believe that the Lord will do just what he said he would do, especially when the proof is in the pudding. Faith the size of a mustard seed will move mountains. If you stand firm on your faith, anything is possible with God.

Hebrews 11:1 says, "Now faith is the substance of things hoped for, the evidence of things not seen." Your faith is not activated until you put your faith in action, because faith without works is dead. Put your faith in action and be determined to finish what you started. I can recall many times when I had to believe God for things that seemed impossible, but with God, all things are possible for them who believe.

Prayer Line: Another Great Move of God

🌹

I am so glad that I am a believer and a fighter. It is important to know God's voice. When the pandemic began, our church was about to start a thirty-day prayer. About three days before we started, the news media was asking everybody to close their church doors. I decided to open a prayer conference phone line for thirty days. I felt that it was time to bring the saints together in prayer.

The prayer line got off to a great start. The word got around very quickly. The theme song was sung every night: "There is a Blessing on This Line Waiting for You." If you believe it, you can receive it. A scripture was read every night on the line. We took prayer requests and offered praise reports every night. Someone would then a sing a song each night. Last but not least, the spoken word came each night with scripture and a topic. We would then close out with a prayer. This prayer phone line grew by leaps and bounds. As I mentioned, the conference call was supposed to last only thirty days. Many church doors were closed. As time passed and we began to approach the end of the thirty-day prayer line, people began to ask me not to shut the conference call down because the prayer line was the only church service available to them. I was truly blessed by these services in many ways. Many people have become a part of this great move of God. Each night, the number of attendees on the conference call continued to grow. We started having everyone announce his or her location when the call ended. The call would end with people signing off from Florida, Alabama, Texas, Georgia, Charleston, and other places. We became one big happy family. We enjoyed praying together, working as a team. We operated like there is no "I" in team.

We had a prayer line conference this year and many people came from all over the United States. I was so excited; I did not know what to do with myself. I finally had a chance to put faces with the voices I heard on the prayer line every night. I was happy when they came but it broke my heart to see them leave. All of them told me what a great time they had. They all talked about how anointed my pulpit was. I am reminded of the Azuza Street Revival that broke out in Los Angeles, California in 1906 and has been going on for over a hundred years. I had a chance to meet so many awesome men and women of God. The prayer conference line never ended, and it is still going strong today. Every night, we call into the conference line for prayer, scripture readings, testimonies, singing, and fellowship. Even on holidays and special occasions, we have enough ministers and prayer warriors in place to lead the conference call. Who knows, this prayer line could go on and grow until Jesus returns.

Prayer Changes Things

After praying with the saints on the prayer line two years ago, I woke up one morning with cramps in my legs and thighs so bad I could hardly bear the pain. My primary doctor gave me some pain medication and two shots. Nothing seemed to help. The doctor then referred me to an orthopedic specialist. After an extensive examination, x-rays, MRIs, and everything else they could think of, they decided that I had a bad disc in my back and the only thing to resolve it would be surgery. The doctor said he would have to remove that bad disc and replace it. The orthopedic specialist explained to me how long I would be in surgery, how long I would be in the hospital, and that I would have to go to a rehab center for a while after the procedure. He further explained that this was a serious surgery for someone my age. It didn't sound like something I wanted to do. I decided to let them put a shot in my back to help the pain cramps. Two days after I had the shots, my legs became very weak. My legs gave way and I fell. To prevent the fall, I stretched out my right arm to keep from falling on my face. All my weight went on my right wrist. I fell in my driveway, bruised my face, split my lip, and broke my wrist. This caused me to seek other options to find a solution to my legs. I decided to get a second opinion. The second doctor said the same thing. I ended up walking with a rolling walker for a while and I later began to use a walking cane. Both doctors said that I would need a walker or a cane.

Unfortunately, my legs did not get any better, as I hoped they would. I fell two other times. I was very unstable on my feet, and my balance was very bad. I needed someone to drive me everywhere I went for a long time. When I arrived at church, someone met me and helped me get out of the car with my belongings. I can remember sitting on the floor of the pulpit because I could not stand to deliver the message on Sunday mornings. I needed someone to help me up the stairs to the pulpit and someone to help me down. Many people prayed and anointed my feet and legs. I know the Bible says in James 5:16, "The effectual fervent prayer of a righteous man availaith much." I was beginning to feel sorry for myself because I could no longer do the things that I loved to do. I could not kneel down to pray. I slipped many times getting in and out of the bathtub. I had to be very careful in my house; I had to make sure I had something to hold on to at all times. I had faith in God, and I did not understand why I had to go through those changes. I did not know when, but I knew that I was going to be healed. I know that God was, is, and always be a healer. Nothing can make me doubt him. I know too much about him.

I thought about how God healed so many people that I prayed for. I was reminded of Isaiah 53:5: "He was wounded for our transgressions. He was bruised for our iniquities; the chastisement of our peace was upon him and by his strips we are healed."

I had to put my faith in action and be determined to trust God no matter what. When I came to that conclusion, I woke up on Easter Sunday morning. I called the person who drove me to church, and I told her that she did not have to drive me to church. I told her that Jesus rose on Easter Sunday morning, and I was going to rise also. I expressed to her that I would drive myself to church that day. The drive to church that day was a risk, but I knew I was not alone, and I knew my God would guide and protect me. By the help of the good Lord, I am still . driving and holding my own. I walk without a walker or a cane. I just did not think I would survive another surgery like that. I learned to trust God no matter what.

I always believed that God would do anything but fail. As far back as I can remember, I held on to faith in God. I suffered many heartaches, disappointments, and offenses, and being pushed aside onto the back burner, so to speak. However, I never lost my faith in God. I always felt that, sooner or later, God would come through for me. I can recall the times when visiting ministers stood in my pulpit and came against things that I believed the Lord would do for the ministry. One preacher said many other people believed God would give them that same building but they could not get it. She said, "What makes you think that you are going to get it?" Hebrew 11:1 says, "Now faith is the substance of things hope for and the evidence of things not seen." I believe I can get anything I want from the Lord.

I Could Never Tell It All

When I thought about all the good things and the bad things, I thought of how God was there to deliver me out of them all. When my mother died and I had to raise my three little sisters and my little brother, God never left us alone. I thank God for strong faith when I did not understand what faith was. I just knew that there is no failure in God. I have the gift of faith. Thank God for the gift. I was reminded of some of the true faith stories in my first two books.

God will reach down and bring you up just when you think you have gone down for the last time. Don't give up on God. Trust God no matter what. I went fishing with some friends on the Edisto River and I fell in the water. They could not get me out. I drifted far away from them, and I could not swim. I went under the water two times. When I came up the last time, there was a limb hanging over the water. My hands touched the limb. I had enough strength to pull myself above the water, and with the help of my friends, I was safe once again. In this case and many others, God has proven to me how faithful he is, how powerful he is, and how true he is to his word that says he will never leave me or forsake me. Many years ago, the Lord was getting me ready for where he was taking me. I can tell anybody: no matter what, trust God. I will never forget the miracle on the Edisto River.

Warning Comes before Destruction

We were happy about paying off our church. We invited everyone to come and celebrate with us. Many people came from all over to help us celebrate. We were making plans to renovate, pave the parking lot, and do some other things. Everyone was excited. I began to hear this still, small voice saying to me, "Greater is coming. Greater is coming." I could not rest because I kept hearing it. I told everyone at the church, No one knew what was about to come. I decided to have a very large banner made. I asked the men of the church to place the banner high across the top of the pulpit.

We praised the Lord for everything. We began to give God the praise for the greater. When visitors came from all over, they wanted to know about the greater that was coming because they thought we knew. About eight months later, while I was still waiting for an understanding about the greater, I began to hear the same still, small voice.

This time, I heard him say, "Fresh start." Just those two words was all I heard. I told everybody that we were going into prayer. I said we were going to ask the Lord to let us know about the "greater is coming" and the "fresh start." We gathered at the church at noon Monday through Friday. Not long after that one week of prayer, we discovered a crack in the ceiling.

The Ceiling Fell In

We did not take the crack seriously. One Sunday evening, we had a program at the church and the program's attendance was graced with many people from other churches. After we went home that night, something happened. One of the members went to the church the next morning. The young man called me and said, "Pastor, you need to come over to the church. The ceiling fell in!" I could never explain what I felt at that moment. I did not want to believe it. I got myself together and drove to the church. When I saw sheet rock, boards, long nails, and dust everywhere, I got weak in my knees. I felt like I was going to faint. I just could not believe my eyes. I could not think about anything other than what I was looking at. When I came to myself, I began to call some of the other members of the church. I believe every one of them was lost for words. Finally, someone had enough courage to say, "Pastor, you know God kept sending us warnings. First, he said, 'Greater is coming,' then he said, 'Fresh start.' Next was the crack in the ceiling, then the ceiling came down." I told everyone that I did not know what God was about to do, but I knew he is up to something. I told them that God does not make mistakes. He is too wise to make mistakes and he is too just to do anything wrong. I told everyone that I could not wait to see what God was about to do for us this time. God is awesome and he doesn't make mistakes. I decided that we would not miss any church services. Our prayer and Bible study classes were scheduled for the very next night. We prayed and gave God thanks for not letting us be in that building when the ceiling fell because we probably would not have lived to tell the story.

I learned to see the goodness of God in all things, even when I don't understand what he is doing. We need to trust God when we can't trace him. The next night, we conducted prayer and Bible study outside on the patio. All of the members came. They wanted to know where our services would be held. Everyone needs to know the voice of the Lord. I was trying to teach and deliver a word from the Lord. Once again, all I could hear was supernatural. I paused for a moment to be sure that I was hearing from the Lord.

The next day, I set out to find a place where we could hold our Sunday services. I was sitting at the traffic light. I was about to go straight through the light, and I heard, "Turn right." The Lord led me to some property that was for sale. I knew about that property, but I thought it was already sold. That property had two church buildings and many other buildings. All I wanted to do was to see if I could lease the smaller church until we could get our church ceiling repaired, but God had other plans. I called the number on the for-sale sign, and someone met me there. He said, "Pastor, the smaller church you called about has problems. Let me show you the larger church." God was trying to tell us something. I called the members together along with my family and we took a supernatural giant step of faith. We had church services in that church one week from the time our ceiling fell in the other church. The Lord is truly blessing us in every service. I believe that the Lord will bless us to pay this church off just like he did for the other church. I am a believer; I take God at his word. I know what the word of the Lord says. Mark 11:24 says, "Therefore, I say unto you what things so ever ye desire when ye pray, believe that ye receive them, and ye shall have them." John 14:14 says, "If ye shall ask anything in my name, I will do it." So says the Lord.

I believe I will always remember going into the woods to sit on that stump. I wish that stump was still there. Sometimes, I drive through that neighborhood thinking about that stump. Many houses have been built there, but I still remember the spot. I believe my gift of faith began in those woods. I was a small child, but I felt like I could have anything I wanted once I made it to that stump. When I came out of those woods, I felt brand new. I felt strong. I felt like I could do anything that my mother wanted me to do. I felt like I was ready for whatever the world had to offer. There is a God who knows it all if you trust him and never doubt. He will bring you out. Believe me when I tell you it has been quite a journey, and it still is. I have experienced many trials and tribulations, but God has delivered me out of them all. I will never forget where God brought me from. I will never forget what he brought me through. I know the Lord to be the truth, the whole truth, and nothing else but the truth. I remember when I could not understand why no one seemed to have faith like I have. One of the ministers in our church told me that I could not expect everybody to have faith like I have. She said it was because no one in the church had suffered and gone through many things like I did. I had to agree with her.

We, the members of the Faith and Action Ministries, are well on our way to a fresh start, and we do believe that greater is coming. We also believe that our setback was a set-up for our comeback.

Printed in the United States
by Baker & Taylor Publisher Services